SOMERSET

SCENES

INCLUDING EXCERPTS

FROM

THE GROCKLES' GUIDE

OTHER BOOKS BY THE SAME AUTHOR ARE LISTED AT THE END OF THIS BOOK

SOMERSET SCENES

TEIL

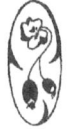

THE THORN PRESS

TABLE OF CONTENTS

SOMERSET, 1970-1985

I started painting after we'd lived on the Somerset Levels for a few years. My children, and making the family self-sufficient in fruit and vegetables, took up all my time until, suddenly, the children became teenagers. I found I had time for other projects.

I've always enjoyed art – drawing, painting, pen and ink – but I've never been keen on painting classes. Nor do I like the smell of oil paints and turpentine. So when I came across the – then – new acrylic paints I was thrilled. Better than that, it was possible to buy the pigments and make up one's own paints by adding the medium oneself. The acrylic medium was available in high gloss, gloss and flat. Wonderful…

Another peculiarity of my efforts at painting was that I do not like easels. I like to paint on the flat, and this is particularly useful for acrylic paints which can be applied thickly, almost like painting in three dimensions. If the canvas – in my case hardboard because I couldn't afford the high prices of canvas at the time – is flat, the paints will not drip. And, because hardboard is a very boring surface with a rather unattractive base colour, I used an underpainting coat in an off white, both to cover the base and to add texture. I like curves; I painted various scrolling curves as a thick undercoat. I hoped this would give some sort of backing to the final painting as well as obliterate the hardboard colour. These undercoats aren't obvious in the final painting, but they do have an effect.

Another method I adopted was to use small, empty, cleaned plastic containers – margarine tubs, cottage cheese containers, anything like that – and put a large blob of paint in the bottom, then cover that with water. The thinning medium for acrylic paints is water, but if you don't mix it in it covers the paint and keeps it from drying out and getting wasted. Paints are also expensive, so this was a handy way not to waste any.

We moved to the Somerset Levels in 1964, to a small village between Wells and Glastonbury. This area is an astonishingly beautiful part of the country, with the added bonus of the Mendip Hills fringing the Levels to prevent the boredom of a never-ending plain.

I love the Moors, as the locals dub the Levels, in all seasons and at all times of the day. And, lucky enough to live in a house perched on a small hillock - a burtle - overlooking the Levels and fringed by the Mendips to the East, I did not want for inspiration.

The paintings in this book are all from that time. I have used material from a book my husband and I published in 1985: *The Grockles' Guide*, a small, illustrated miscellany of local Somerset words and phrases still in use during that period. The excerpts seem an appropriate way to describe some of the paintings.

DEDICATION

TO MY CHILDREN - MADELEINE, COLIN & RICHARD -
WHO SHARE MY LOVE FOR THE SOMERSET LEVELS.

SOMERSET

THE NAME FOR THE COUNTY OF SOMERSET IS SAID TO COME FROM THE WORD SUMORSEATE - TAKEN FROM OLD ENGLISH AND MEANING THE LAND OF THE SUMMER PEOPLE. BEFORE THE AREA WAS DRAINED IT WAS VIRTUALLY UNINHABITABLE IN THE WINTER MONTHS.

THE SWEET TRACK AT SHAPWICK HAS BEEN DATED TO 3806 BC, SHOWING THAT THE MARSHES WERE INHABITED FROM A VERY EARLY PERIOD. THE LAKE VILLAGE, NEAR GLASTONBURY, WAS BUILT IN ABOUT 300 BC, WITH SETTLERS THERE UNTIL AROUND 100 AD.

THE LAND WAS DRAINED IN VARIOUS WAYS AT DIFFERENT TIMES. THE DUTCH, IN PARTICULAR, WERE BRILLIANT AT DRAINING THEIR OWN LAND AND BROUGHT THEIR EXPERTISE TO OTHER COUNTRIES.

AND THE NAME OF THE BATTLE OF SEDGEMOOR, WHICH TOOK PLACE IN 1685 AD AT WESTONZOYLAND, NEAR BRIDGWATER, IS A CLUE TO THE VEGETATION - THE COARSE SEDGE GRASSES - GROWING ON THE LEVELS AT THAT TIME.

CIDER APPLE ORCHARD IN BLOOM

THERE ARE STILL A FEW ORCHARDS IN RURAL SOMERSET, THOUGH THE BULK OF CIDER APPLES ARE NOW GROWN IN FRANCE. UNLIKE THE EATING VARIETIES OF APPLE, OLD SOMERSET CIDER APPLE ORCHARDS HAVE GNARLED TRUNKS AND BRANCHES, AND ARE ALLOWED TO GROW UNCHECKED. THEY SPRAWL AND LEAN, AS THOUGH DRUNK ON THEIR OWN CROP.

SOMERSET CIDER IS WELL KNOWN, CALLED SCRUMPY BY THE LOCALS. IT LOOKS INNOCENT ENOUGH, BUT EVEN A GLASS OR TWO WILL HAVE A NOTICEABLE EFFECT.

SCRUMPY

THIS IS THE TRADITIONAL FARMHOUSE CIDER, STILL AND NOT FIZZY, UNIQUE IN CHARACTER, AND A DRINK FOR WHICH SOMERSET IS FAMOUS. SCRUMPLING IS LISTED AS A SMALL APPLE WHICH NEVER REACHES PERFECTION, WHILE SCRUMP IS A WEST COUNTRY WORD MEANING TO SCRUNCH.

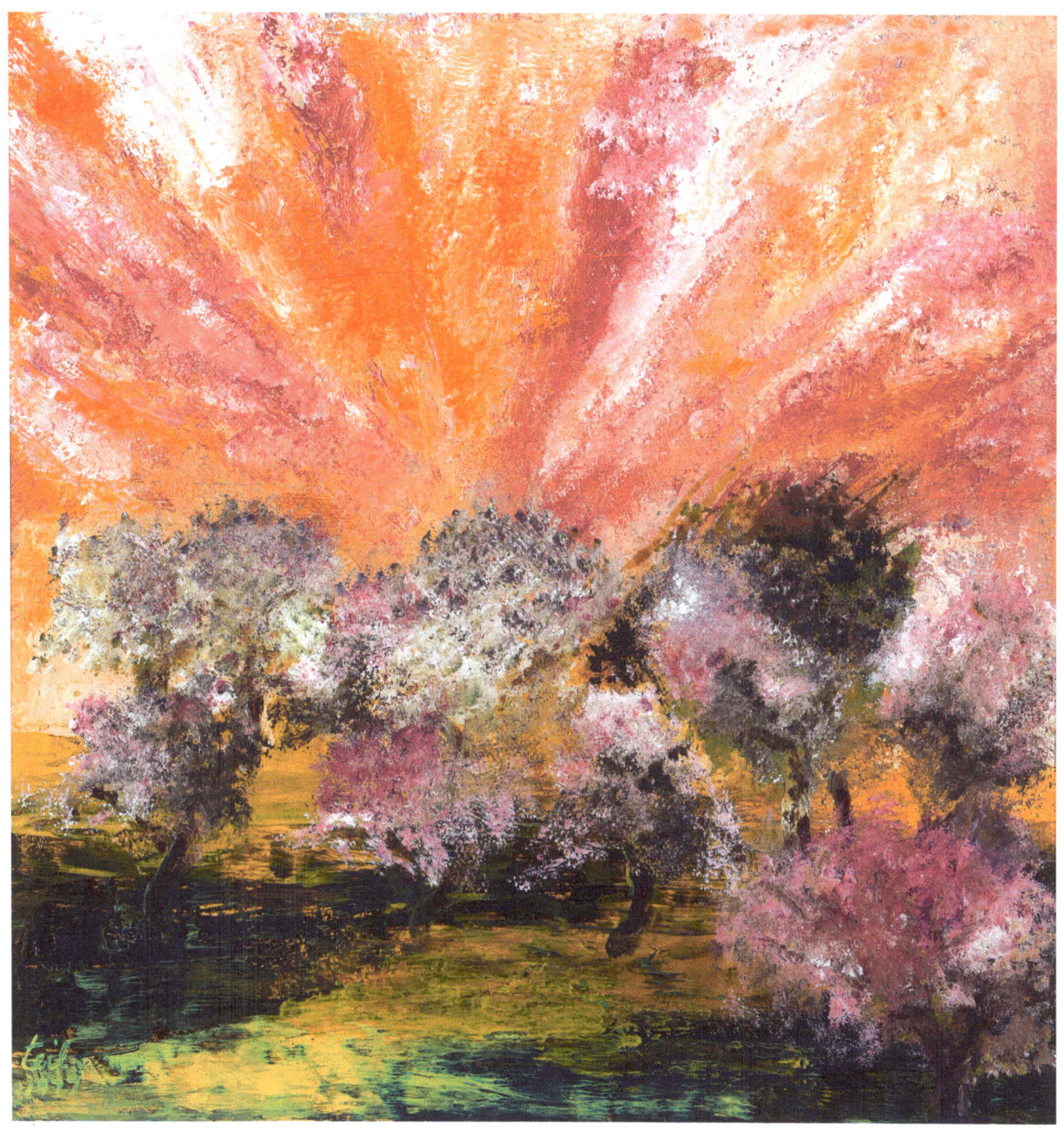

HUNTING COWS

One of the pitfalls of driving on the moor roads is that the farmers move their milch cows along these roads at milking time.

Large herds of stolid animals, their udders full to bursting, their rear sides moving slowly ahead, plod sedately and heavily along the moor roads.

It isn't sensible to try to pass them; both the cows and the farmers take exception to that...

TO HUNT

With reference to cattle, to hunt means to walk a herd of milch cows or other farm animals from one place to another along the moor roads or droves.

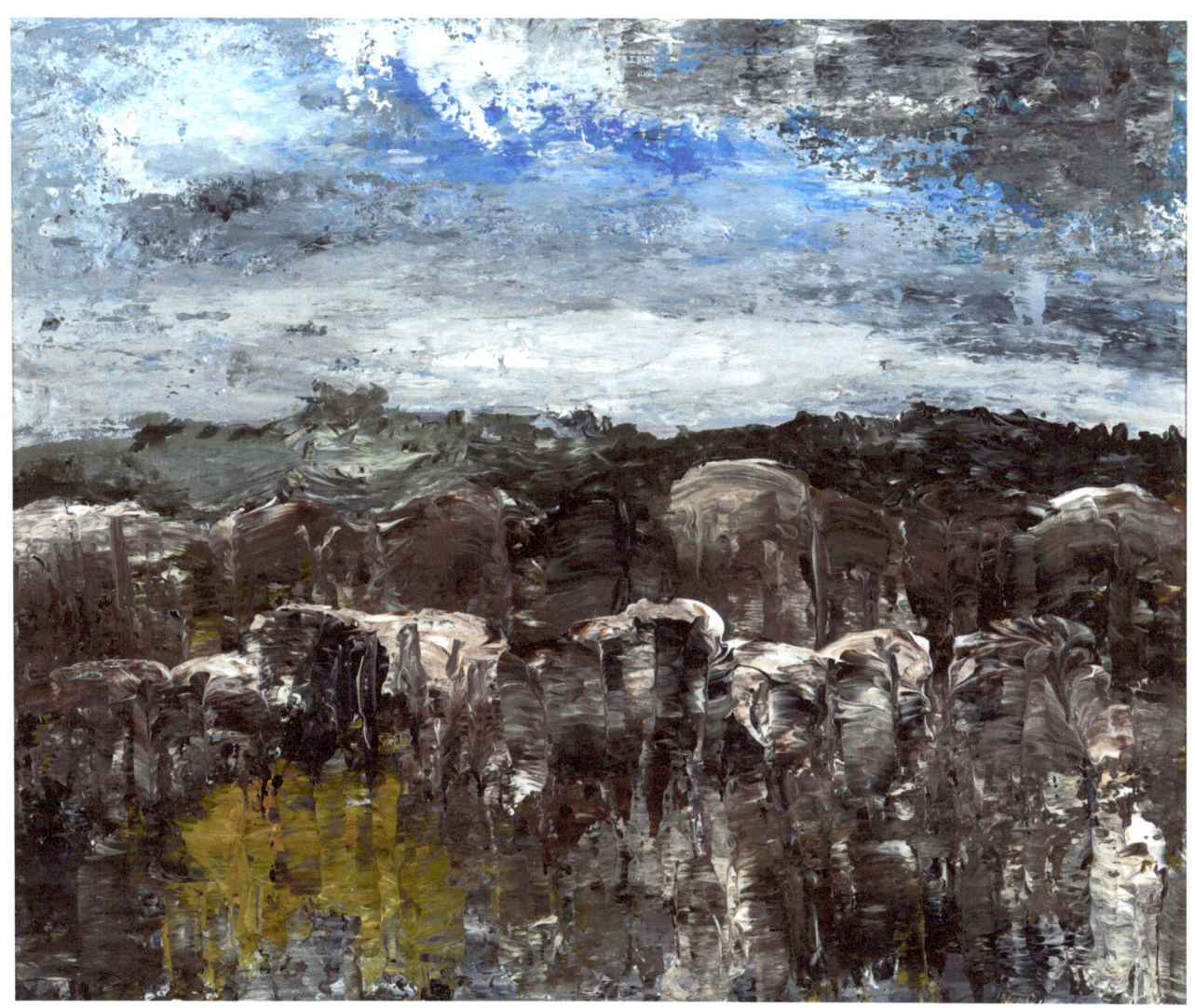

FARM COTTAGES

SMALL, STONE-BUILT COTTAGES AND SHEDS SPRAWL OVER THE
COUNTRYSIDE. FARM BUILDINGS, NOT SUBJECT TO PLANNING
PERMISSION, APPEAR UNLOVELY SCATTERED OVER THE LEVELS.
THE FIVE-BAR GATES, AND THE RHYNES OR DITCHES AT THE
BOUNDARIES, KEEP CATTLE OR SHEEP IN THE FIELDS.

LEVELS

AS IN SOMERSET LEVELS, THE LOWLANDS WHICH STRETCH ACROSS THE
CENTRAL SOMERSET PLAIN. NOT ACTUALLY LEVEL, OF COURSE, BUT
GLASTONBURY TOR, WHICH IS NOT A VERY LARGE HILL, IS A LANDMARK
FOR MILES, DEMONSTRATING HOW FLAT THE LAND REALLY IS.

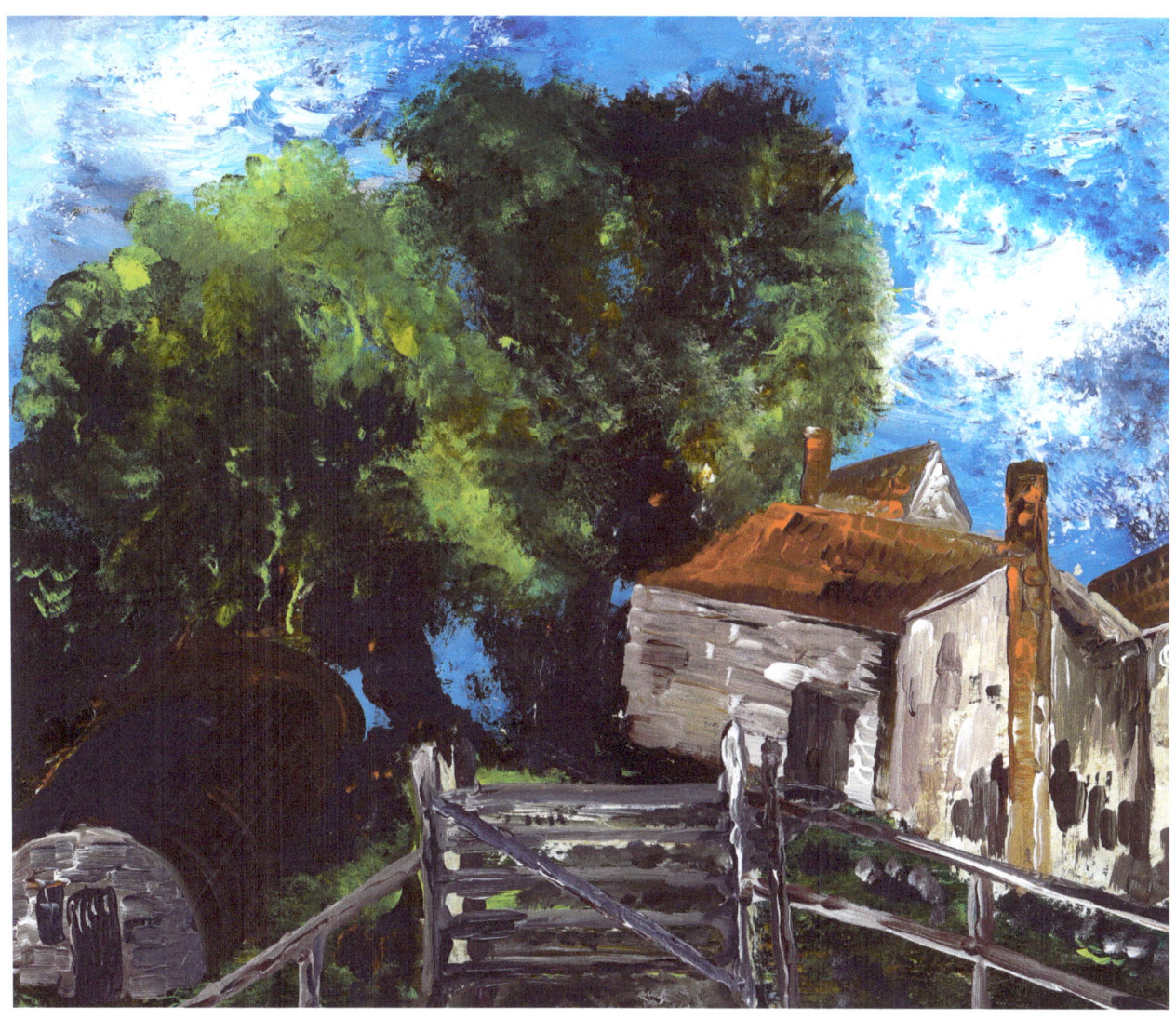

THE FLOODED LEVELS

FLOODS ARE A FACT OF LIFE ON THE SOMERSET LEVELS. IN SPITE OF
RHYNES - DITCHES - LINING THE ROADS AND DRAINING INTO DRAINS
AND RIVERS, THE LEVELS STILL FLOOD AS SOON AS IT RAINS FOR ANY
LENGTH OF TIME. THAT'S WHEN THE MOORS MERGE WITH THE SKY...

THE FLOODS MAY BE A NUISANCE TO FARMERS AND THEIR ANIMALS,
BUT THEY ARE BEAUTIFUL. THE LEAVES SHIMMER, THE SKY REFLECTS
BLUE, GREY AND YELLOW ONTO GREEN.

RHYNES

A RHYNE, OR RHINE, USUALLY PRONOUNCED 'REEN', IS A MAN-
MADE CHANNEL FOR RECEIVING WATER TO DRAIN THE SURROUNDING
LOWLANDS. THE WORD IS THE SAME ONE THAT REFERS TO THE WELL-
KNOWN GERMAN RIVER, THE RHINE.
COMPARE OLD ENGLISH RYNE, A FLOW, AND GERMAN RONNE, A
CHANNEL.
THE WORD DITCH IS OFTEN USED TO REFER TO SMALL RHINES, BUT
DITCHES ARE STATIC AND RHYNES FLOW INTO RIVERS OR DRAINS.

8

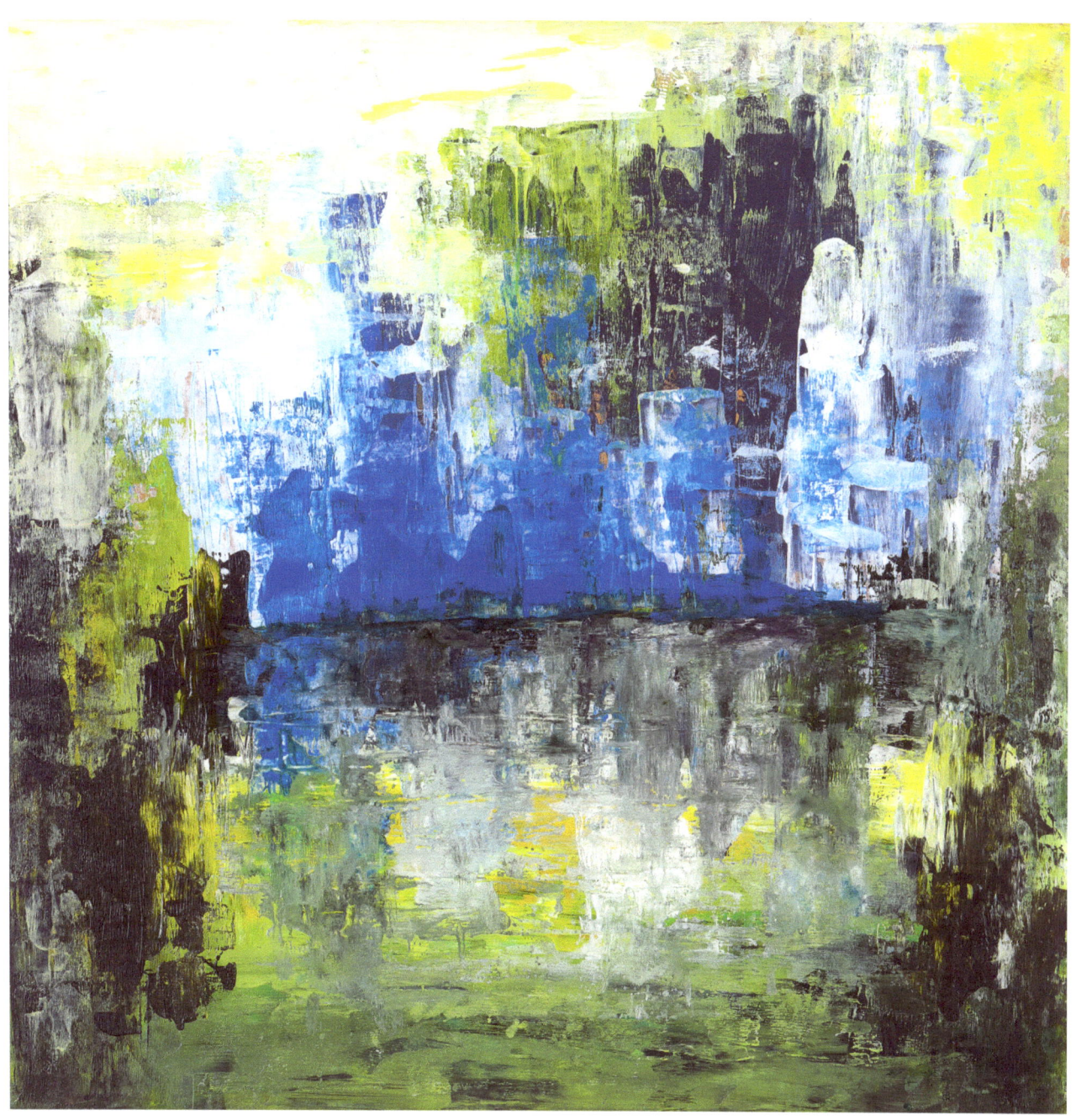

9

MOORLAND TREES

THE LEVELS FILL THE HORIZON WITH ENDLESS GREENS MERGING INTO
THE BLUE OF THE SKY ON A SUNNY DAY.

BUT THE OCCASIONAL TREE STANDS OUT - AND NOT JUST WILLOWS.
SELF-SOWN APPLE AND RUSSET BEECH MANAGE TO HOLD THEIR OWN
AGAINST THE TIDE OF SEDGE AND GRASS, DEFEATING THE CONSTANT
DEPREDATIONS OF SHEEP, CATTLE AND THE HOMICKY FARMER DRIVING
AN UNCARING TRACTOR.

HOMICKY

THE LEVELS ARE FULL OF HOMICKY - CLUMSY OR AWKWARD - CATTLE
BENT ON DESTROYING THE VEGETATION, AS WELL AS FARM WORKERS
WHO SEE TREES AS GETTING IN THEIR WAY.
ALSO USED WERE BACK-HANDED, CACK-HANDED, CLUMBLE-FISTED,
GAMMY-HANDED, LEFT-HANDED, MUZZLE-HANDED, SCAMMISH-HANDED
AND SCRAMMY-HANDED.
THIS LENGTHY LIST OF WORDS STILL IN USE SHOWS HOW RURAL
SOMERSET WAS AT THE TIME.

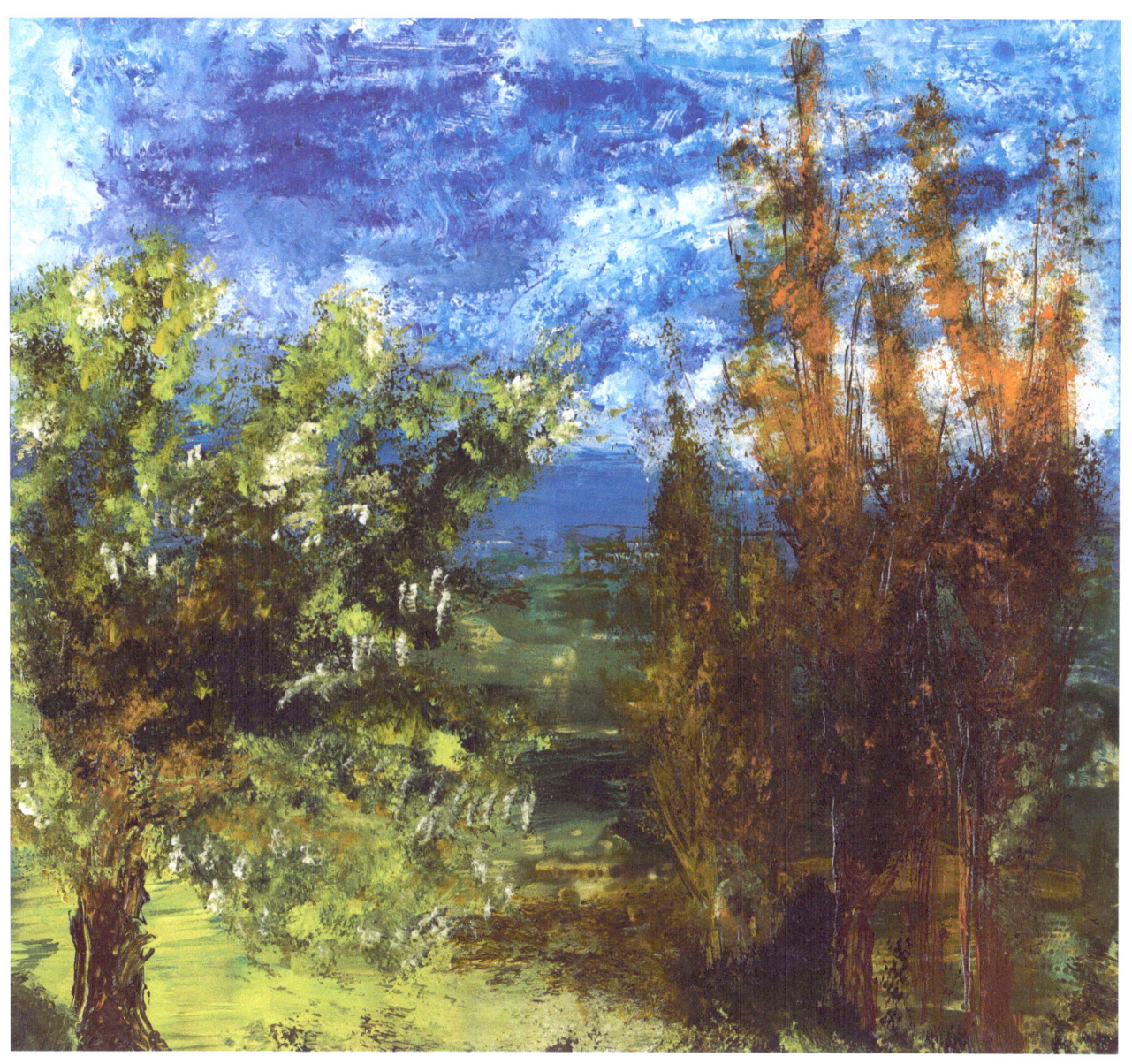

GLASTONBURY TOR

THE TOR, WITH ITS TOWER REMINDING US OF THE ATROCITIES
COMMITTED DURING HENRY VIII'S REIGN, STANDS MAJESTIC IN ALL
WEATHERS, IN ALL SEASONS.

THIS PAINTING WAS DONE ON A BLEAK WINTER'S DAY, SHOWING THE
MILLING CLOUDS AND THE BARE WILLOWS LINING THE RHYNES.

TOR

THE WORD TOR IS COMMON IN SOUTH WESTERN PLACE NAMES,
REFERRING TO A HILL OR HIGH ROCK. SO, IN GLASTONBURY TOR, IT
REFERS TO THE HILL AND NOT TO THE TOWER ON THE TOP.
FROM OLD ENGLISH 'TORR', A ROCK, A ROCKY OUTCROP, A ROCKY
PEAK. THIS WORD GOES BACK TO A ROOT MEANING BULGE OR BELLY.
SO, APPLIED TO THE LANDSCAPE, A TOR IS A BULGING HILL.

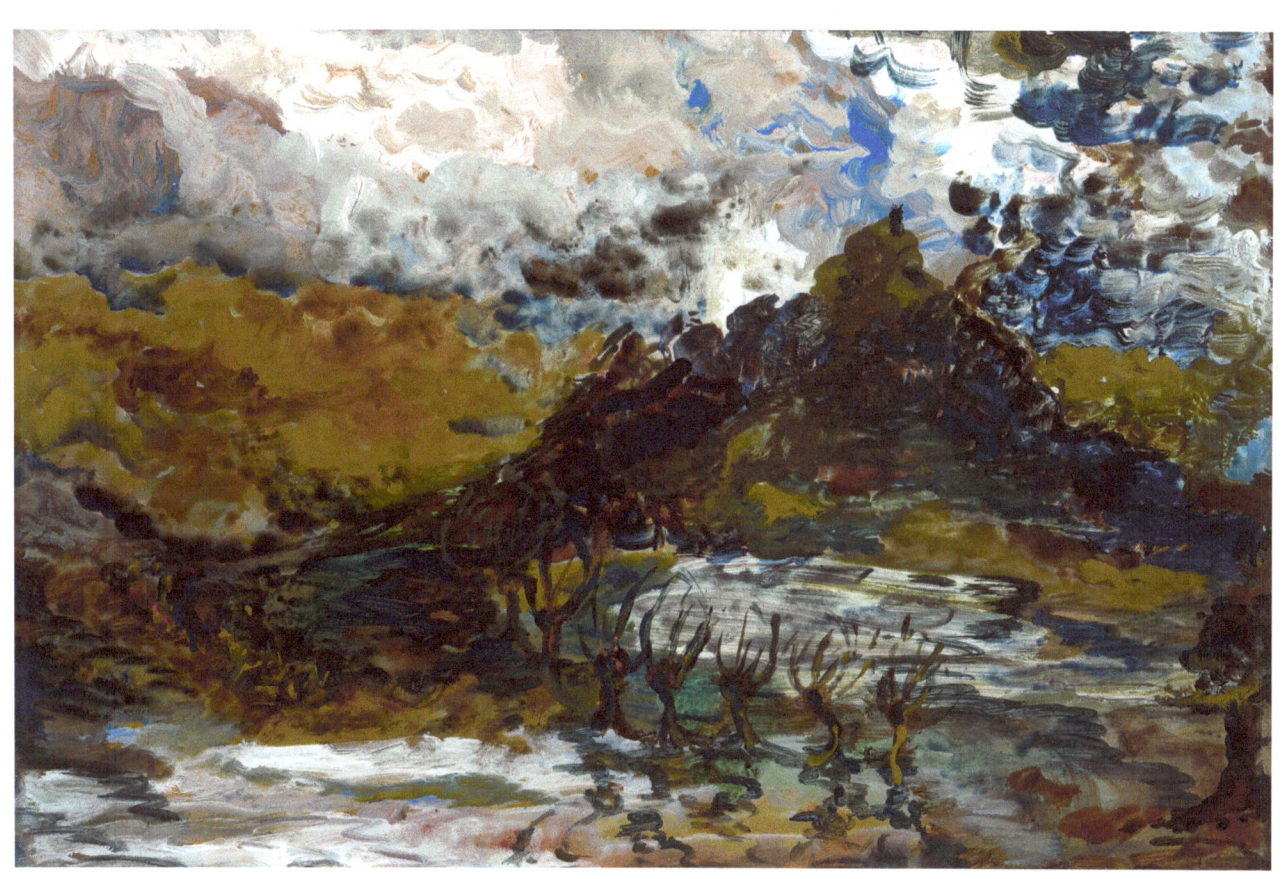

DROVE WITH TREES

SURPRISINGLY, THERE ARE SMALL HILLOCKS, SOMETIMES CALLED BURTLES, ALL OVER THE MOORS, MORE OBVIOUS IF YOU WALK ALONG THE DROVES. THEY MAY HAVE BEEN THERE ORIGINALLY, BUT MORE LIKELY THEY ARE MAN-MADE. ONE JUST OUTSIDE GLASTONBURY, NOW NO MORE, WAS THE SITE FOR THE ANNUAL GLASTONBURY FAYRE.

DROVE

A DROVE IS A TRACK OR PATH, ESPECIALLY ONE ALONG WHICH CATTLE, OR OTHER FARM ANIMALS, ARE DRIVEN. IN EFFECT THEY ARE GREEN LANES, THAT IS UNTARMACKED SURFACES ROADS, LEADING OFF THE PUBLIC HIGHWAYS.
TO DROVE INVOLVES 'DRIVING' THE ANIMALS ALONG SUCH TRACKS. HUNT HAS A SIMILAR MEANING.

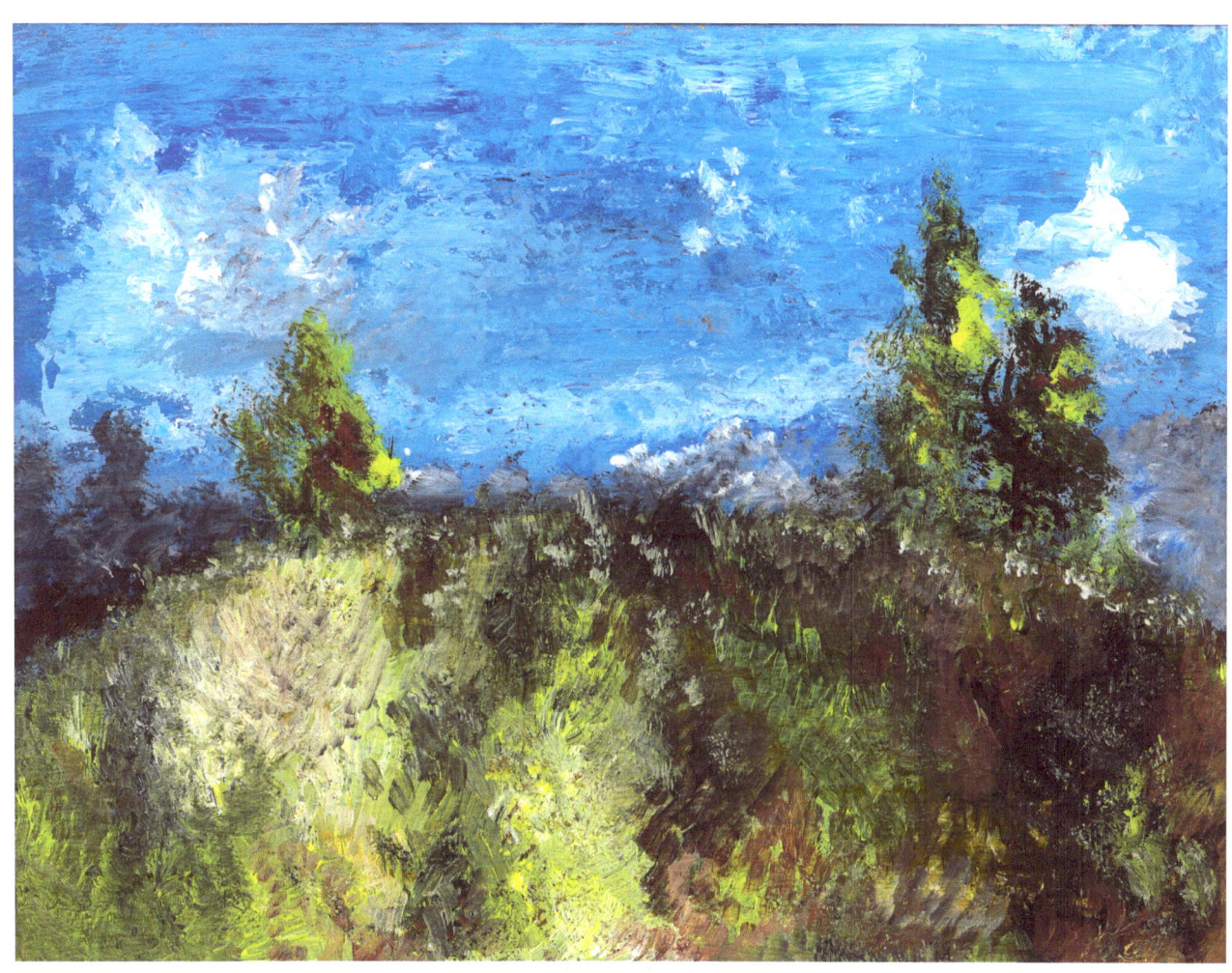

PUSSY WILLOW
SALIX DAPHNOIDES AGLAIA (VIOLET WILLOW)

THE RHYNES, NOT UNEXPECTEDLY, ARE LINED WITH WILLOWS TO KEEP THE BANKS FROM FALLING IN AND TO GIVE AN EDGE TO THE MOORLAND ROADS.

THIS PARTICULAR WILLOW IS NOT A NATIVE, BUT IT GROWS WELL IN SOMERSET SOIL. IT IS BEAUTIFUL IN ALL SEASONS - THE BRANCHES SHINE VIOLET/RED AGAINST THE BLUE OR GREY WINTER SKIES, THE 'PUSSIES' ARE LARGER THAN USUAL, AND THE GLORIOUS YELLOW TASSELS LATER IN SPRING ARE A SIGHT TO BEHOLD.

THIS SHRUB IS ALSO A BRILLIANT POLLINATOR FOR ORCHARDS.

WITHY

A WITHY IS A WILLOW TREE OR OSIER. WITHIES ARE NOT ONLY A FAMILIAR AND LOVELY COMPONENT OF THE LEVELS, THEY ARE GROWN FOR USE IN CRAFTS SUCH AS BASKET-MAKING.

IT IS INTERESTING TO NOTE THAT WITHYWIND IS THE LOCAL NAME USED FOR BINDWEED - CONVOLVULUS ARVENSIS - WITH ITS BEAUTIFUL FLOWERS BUT PESKY WINDING STALKS.

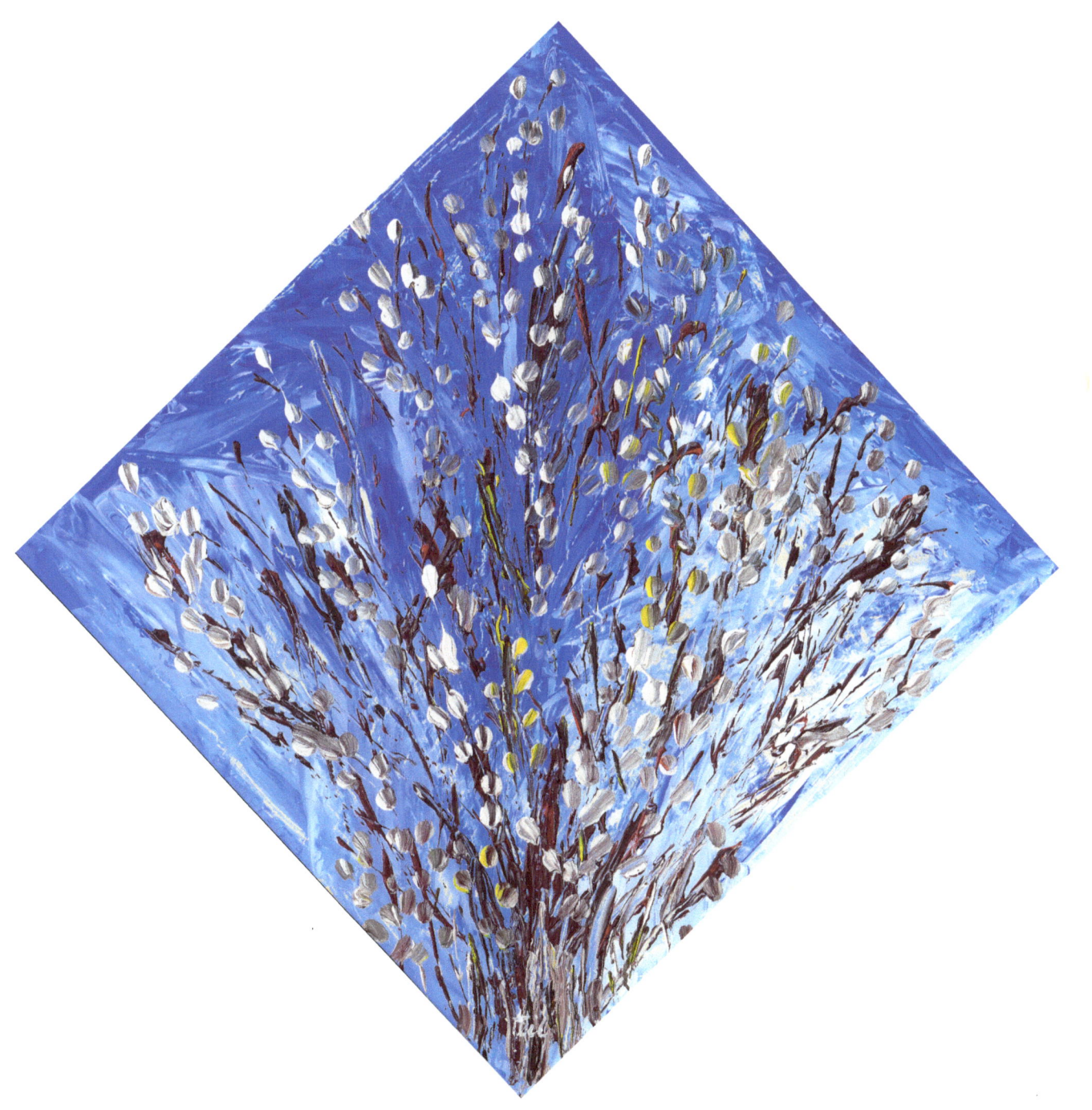

17

THE WIND IN THE WILLOWS

Because the Levels and Moors are so flat the wind tends to
sweep across them unrestrained.
The willows bend gracefully with the wind,
their small, narrow leaves and willowy branches perfectly
suited to coping with the blasts.

BURTLE

These are some slightly raised areas across the Levels,
themselves only about six metres above sea level.

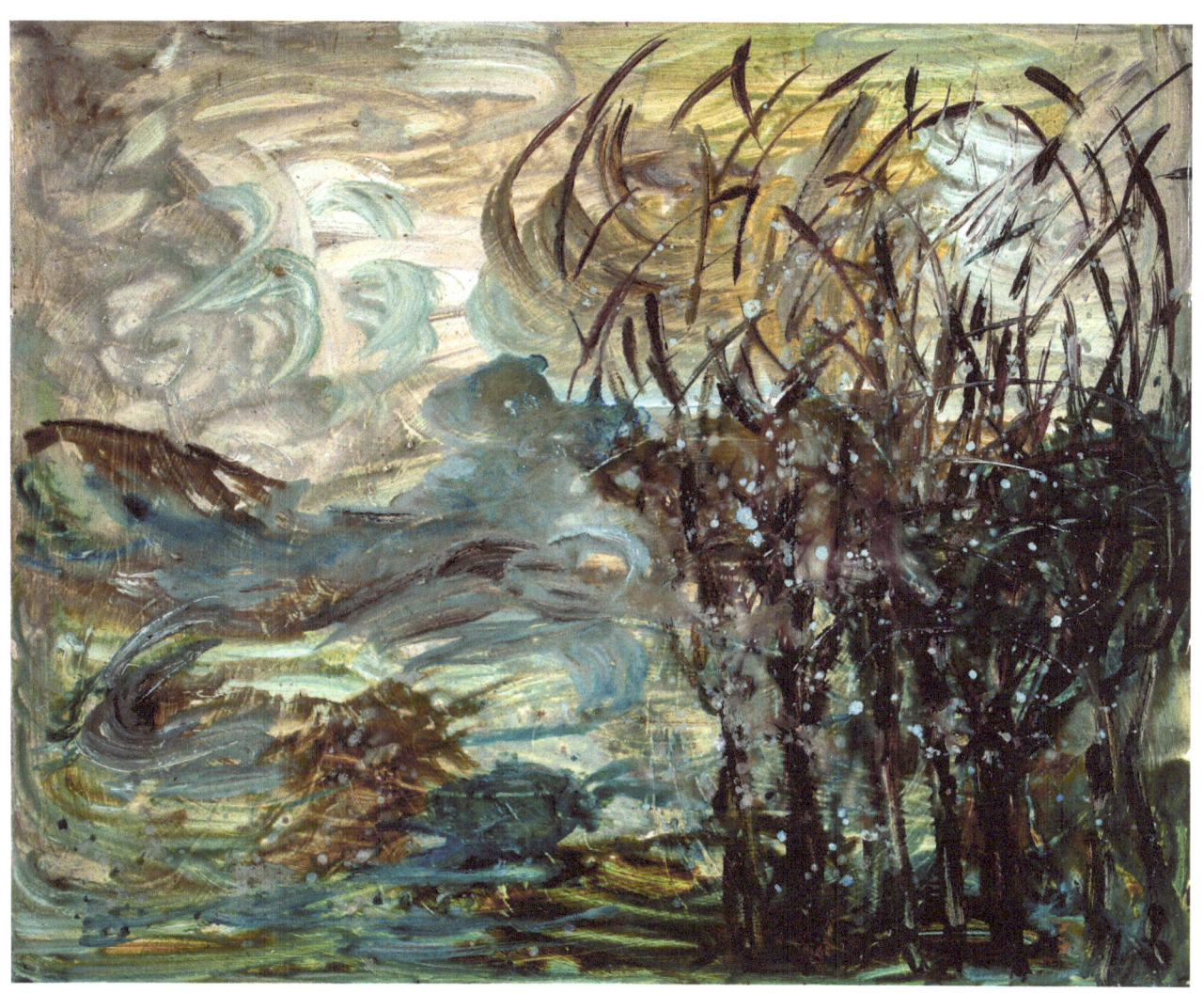

19

A ROAD ACROSS THE MOOR

THE ROADS ACROSS THE MOOR HAVE RHYNES ON BOTH SIDES AND ARE FRINGED WITH WILLOWS. WHEN FULLY GROWN THE BRANCHES OFTEN ARCH OVER THE ROAD, MAKING A CANOPY OF GREENERY IN SPRING AND SUMMER.
THE WILLOWS ARE POLLARDED - THAT IS THE BRANCHES SPROUTING FROM THE TRUNK ARE PRUNED BACK - EVERY COUPLE OF YEARS TO PREVENT THE TREES FROM BECOMING TOP-HEAVY.

THE MOOR

THE SOMERSET LEVELS STRETCH ALONG THE WESTERN COASTLINE OF THE COUNTY. THEY ARE FORMED OF CLAY BELT, AND ARE ONLY SOME SIX METRES ABOVE SEA LEVEL
THE MOORS - ORIGINALLY SEDGEMOORS BEFORE THEY WERE TURNED INTO PERMANENT PASTURE - ARE INLAND FLOOD PLAINS, AND A FEW FEET BELOW THE LEVELS IN HEIGHT.
THE TERMS MOOR AND LEVELS TEND TO BE USED INTERCHANGEABLY.

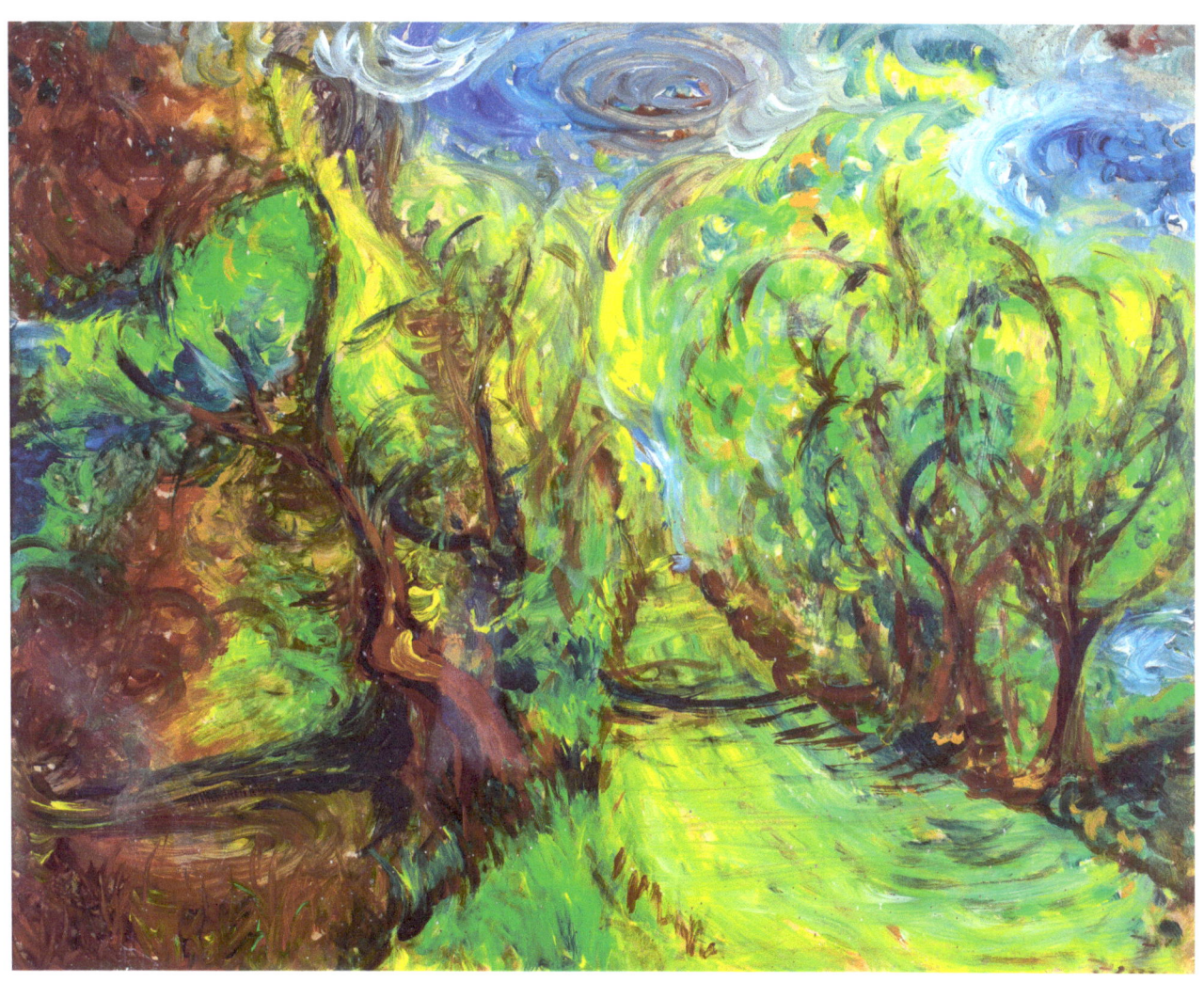

BUTTERCUPS

**A FIELD OF BUTTERCUPS GLOWS IN THE DISTANCE, THE GLORIOUS
YELLOW SHINING AGAINST THE GREEN OF THE PASTURE.
THE POLLARDED WILLOWS IN THE FOREGROUND ARE JUST BEGINNING
TO SPROUT NEW BRANCHES**

PLOUGH-GROUNDS

**PLOUGH-GROUNDS ARE TILLED FIELDS, ARABLE LAND, OR ANY
CULTIVATED LAND RECLAIMED FROM PERMANENT PASTURE OR
SEDGEMOOR. SEDGE IS A GRASS-LIKE PLANT WITH VERY COARSE STEMS
WHICH GROWS WILD ON MOORLAND.**

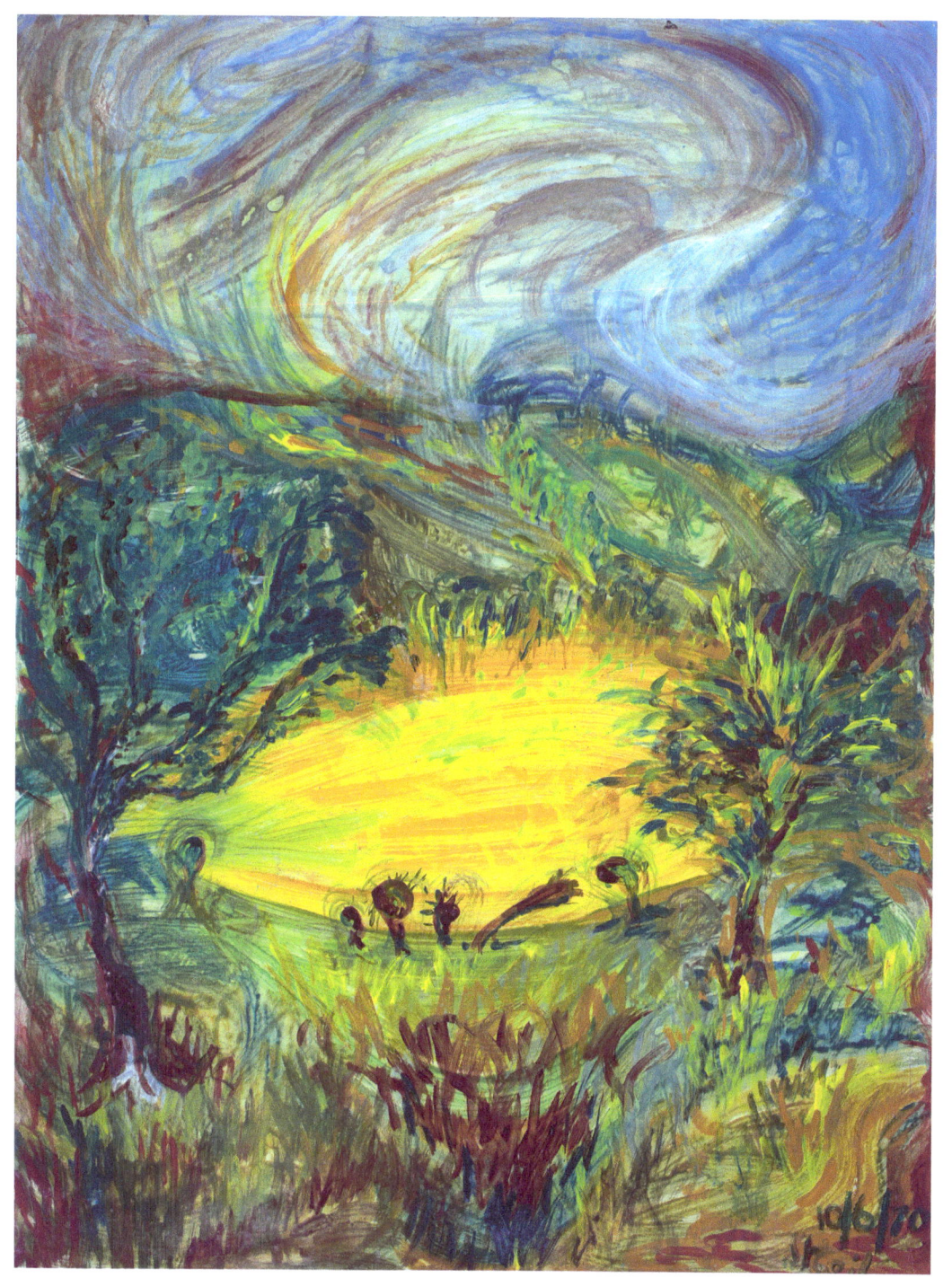

23

MACKEREL SKY

BECAUSE THERE IS A 360° HORIZON ON THE LEVELS THE SKY SCAPE IS
OFTEN AS INTERESTING AS THE LANDSCAPE BELOW IT.
HERE THE MACKEREL SKY SHOWS IN ALL ITS GLORY.

DRAINS

THIS DOESN'T REFER TO THE DOMESTIC PIPE FOR DRAINING WASTE
WATER BUT TO THE SUBSTANTIAL, MAN-MADE, CROSS-COUNTRY
CHANNELS. A DRAIN IS NOT, LIKE A CANAL, USED FOR TRANSPORT, BUT
IS THE RECIPIENT OF WATER FROM THE SMALLER, LAND-DRAINING
DITCHES AND RHYNES.

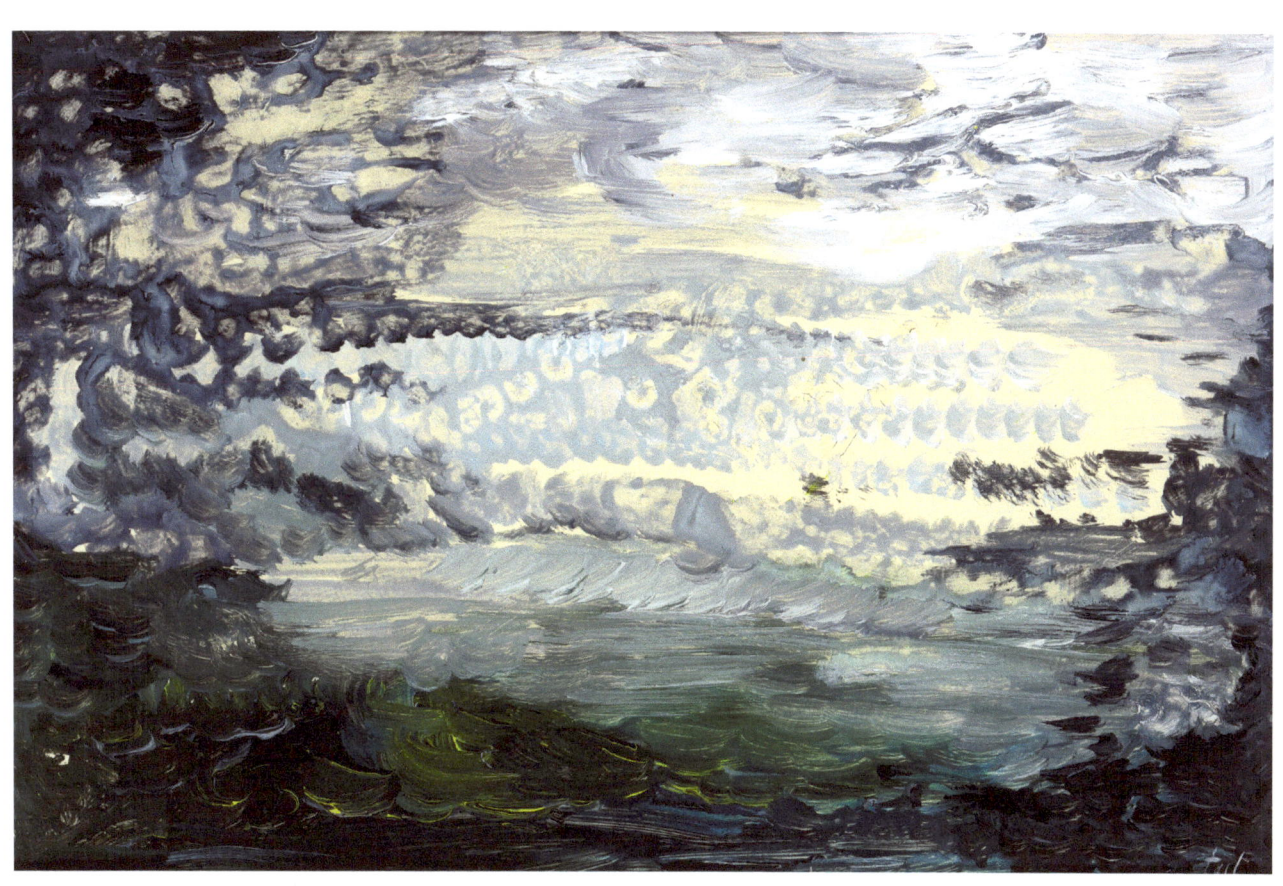

SUNSET IN KING'S CASTLE WOOD

KING'S CASTLE WOOD IS UPALONG, NOT FAR FROM WELLS, THE SMALLEST CITY IN ENGLAND. EVERY NOW AND AGAIN IT IS FUN TO GET AWAY FROM THE LEVELS AND ENJOY THE WOODLANDS OF THE MENDIP HILLS.

UPALONG, DOWNALONG

UPALONG MEANS ALONG, TOWARDS, OR NEAR - ALL IN A GENERALLY UPWARD DIRECTION FROM WHERE THE SPEAKER IS.
DOWNALONG MEANS ALONG, TOWARDS OR NEAR - ALL IN A GENERALLY DOWNWARD DIRECTION FROM WHERE THE SPEAKER IS.

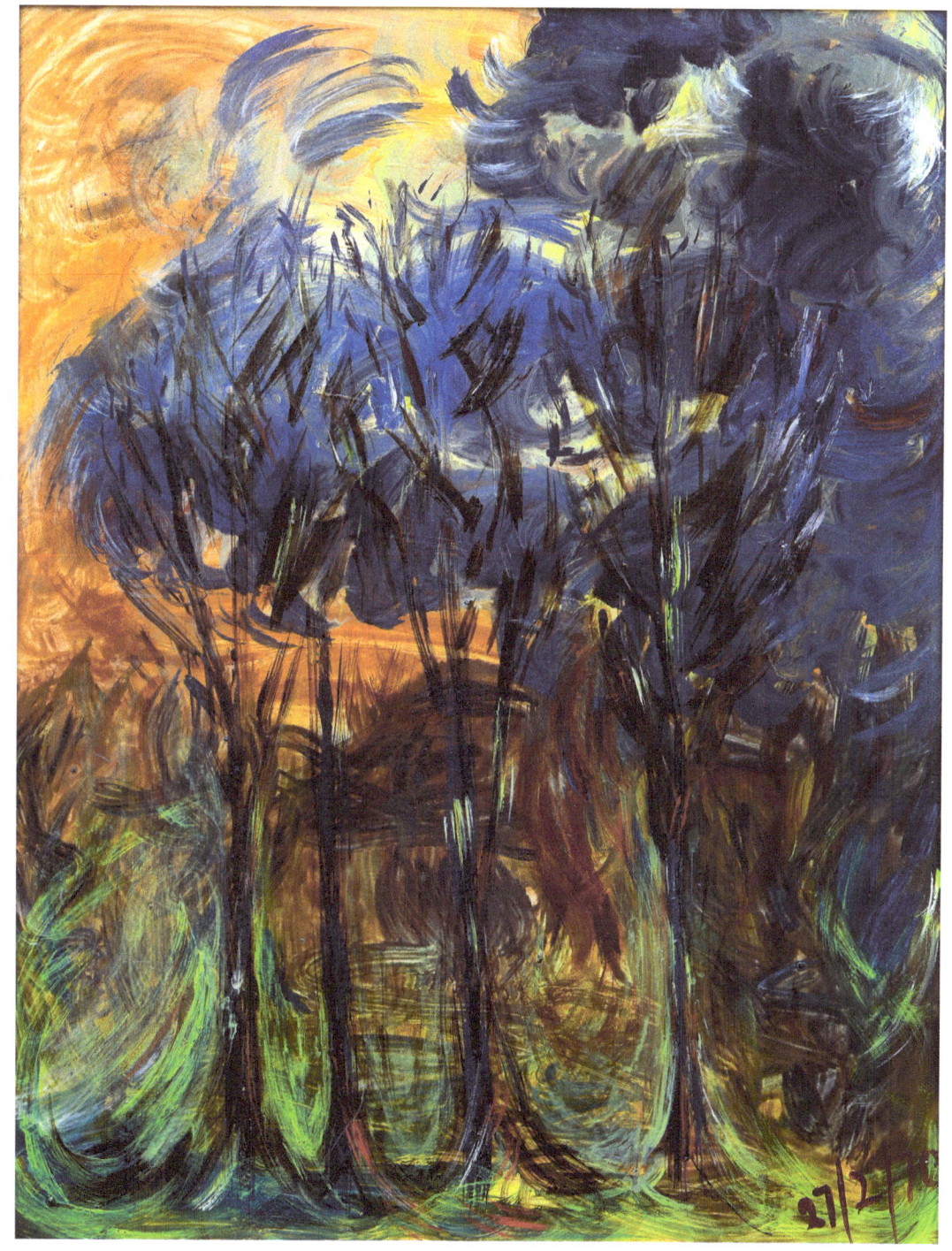

LATE AUTUMN IN THE GROUNDS

OUR HOUSE HAD A LARGE GARDEN, SO TO DIFFERENTIATE OUR LAND FROM THE WIDE SPACES BEYOND WE PLANTED TREES. THEIR GLORIOUS AUTUMN COLOURS WERE BOTH A DELIGHT AND A REAL CONTRAST TO THE CONSTANT GREENERY BEYOND OUR GARDEN.

GROUNDS

GROUNDS ARE CULTIVATED LAND AS OPPOSED TO THE PERPETUAL PASTURES OF THE MOORS.

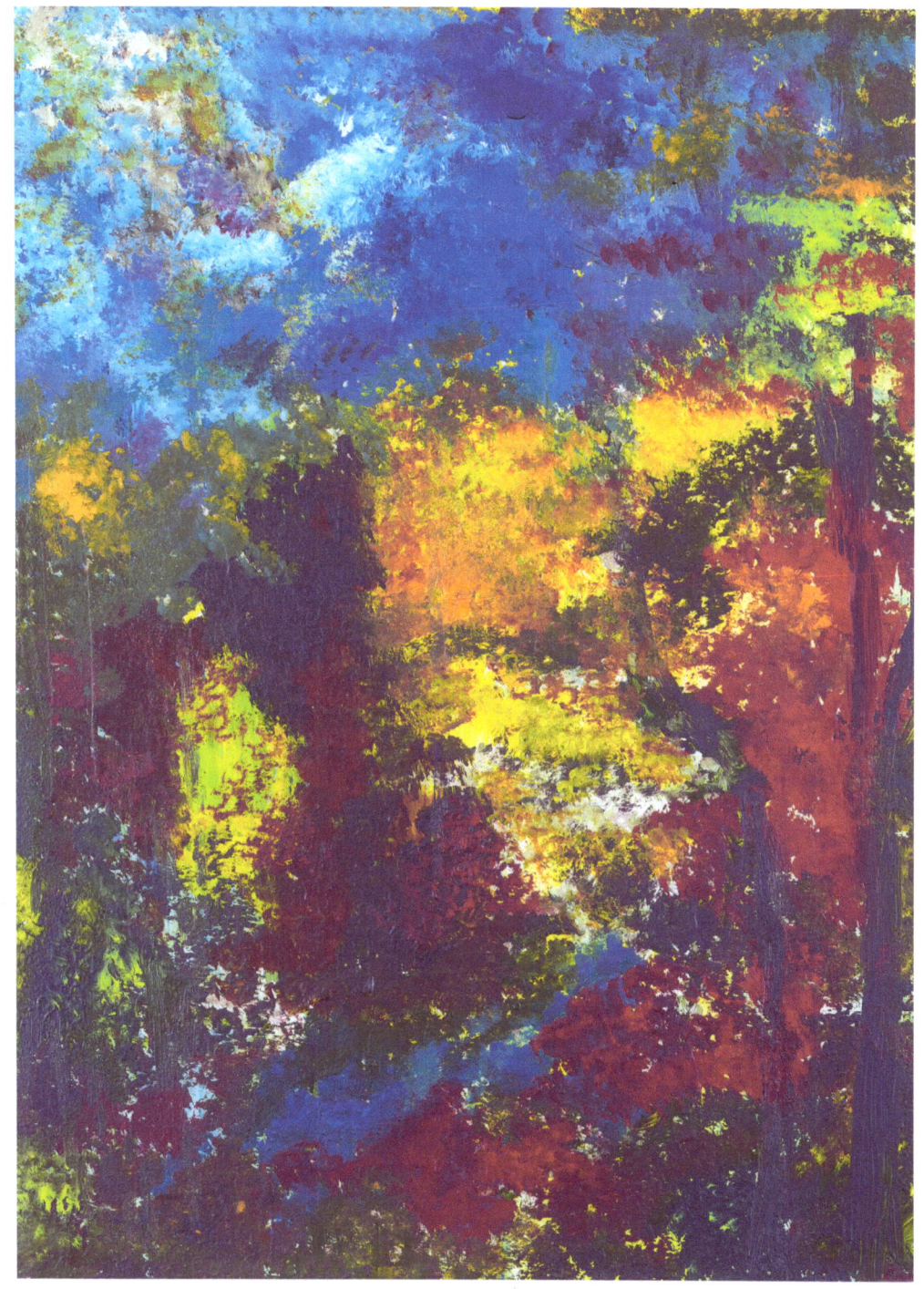

FLOODS AT DIMSEY DARK

THE FLOODED MOORS ARE ALWAYS A FASCINATING SIGHT. THE COLOURS CHANGE DRAMATICALLY, DEPENDING ON THE LIGHT IN THE SKY, THE TIME OF DAY, THE TIME OF YEAR.
THIS PICTURE SHOWS THE REFLECTION OF WHITE CLOUDS EVEN THOUGH THE SUN HAS ALMOST SET.

DIMSEY, DIMSEY DARK

THIS IS THE LOCAL WORD FOR TWILIGHT OR DUSK, AND CAN ALSO MEAN MURKY.
'IT BE GETTING DIMSEY.'
ALSO DUMCEY, DUMCEY DARK.

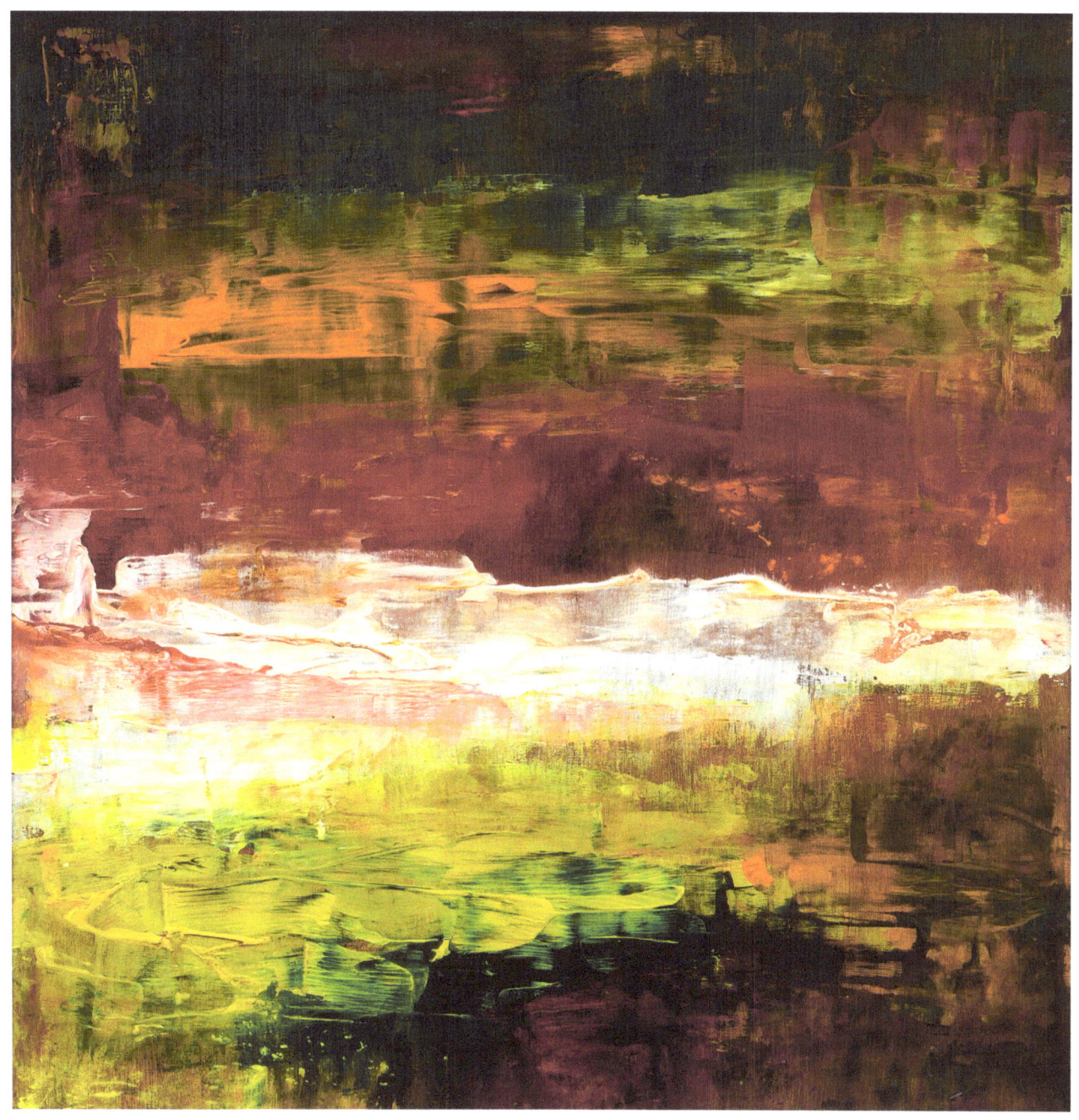

TURKEY OAK BARK

SOMETIMES IT'S WORTH GETTING UP CLOSE: THERE WAS AN ANCIENT
TURKEY OAK IN OUR GARDEN, TOPPLED BY THE UNEXPECTED
HURRICANE OF 1987.
THIS IS MY VISION OF ITS WIDE - FALLING ABROAD - APPARENTLY
STURDY, TRUNK.
THE PAINTING IS A GREAT REMINDER OF ITS MAJESTIC PAST, AS WELL
AS THE FRAGILITY OF ALL LIFE.

FALLING ABROAD

GETTING STOUT, RUNNING TO FAT, LARGER THAN IS GOOD FOR THE PERSON,
PLANT OR ANIMAL.

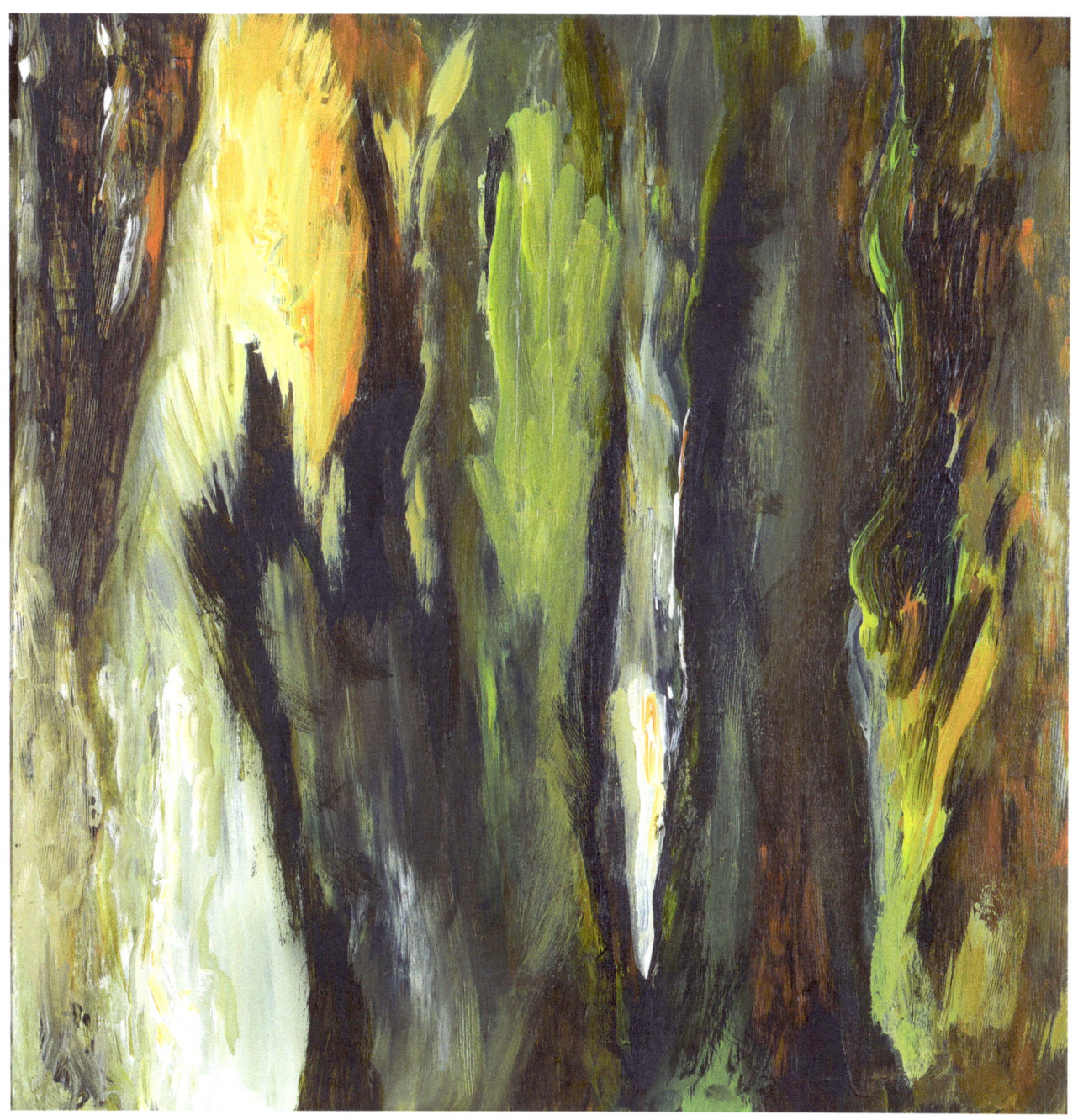

33

THE GLASTONBURY THORN

THIS IS CRATAEGUS MONOGYNA PRAECOX, A VARIANT OF THE
NATIVE HAWTHORN, AND FAMOUS FOR FLOWERING AT CHRISTMAS.
A FLOWERING SPRAY USED TO BE CUT EVERY YEAR FROM THE TREE
OUTSIDE ST JOHN'S CHURCH, IN GLASTONBURY, AND SENT TO THE
QUEEN. UNFORTUNATELY THE TREE WAS BLOWN DOWN IN A GALE.
THIS PLANT IS ALSO KNOWN AS THE HOLY THORN.

THE TREE IS UNUSUAL IN THAT IT BLOOMS IN MID WINTER, BURSTING
INTO GREEN LEAF AND FLOWER, WITH THE SUMMER SCENT OF MAY,
AND CARRYING FLOWER AND FRUIT AT THE SAME TIME.

THE THORN PRESS

FIRST ESTABLISHED IN 1979, IN GODNEY, NEAR GLASTONBURY,
THE THORN PRESS TAKES ITS NAME FROM THE GLASTONBURY THORN,
SAID TO HAVE SPROUTED WHEN JOSEPH OF ARIMATHEA VISITED
WEARYALL HILL, JUST BELOW GLASTONBURY TOR.
HE THRUST HIS STAFF INTO THE GROUND, AND BY THE NEXT
MORNING THE STAFF HAD TAKEN ROOT AND BECOME A THORN BUSH
NOW KNOWN AS THE HOLY THORN. THIS SPECIES OF THORN FLOWERS
TWICE A YEAR: ONCE ON 'OLD WOOD', LIKE ALL OTHER THORN TREES,
THEN AGAIN ON 'NEW' WOOD, AROUND CHRISTMAS.

A Glastonbury Thorn

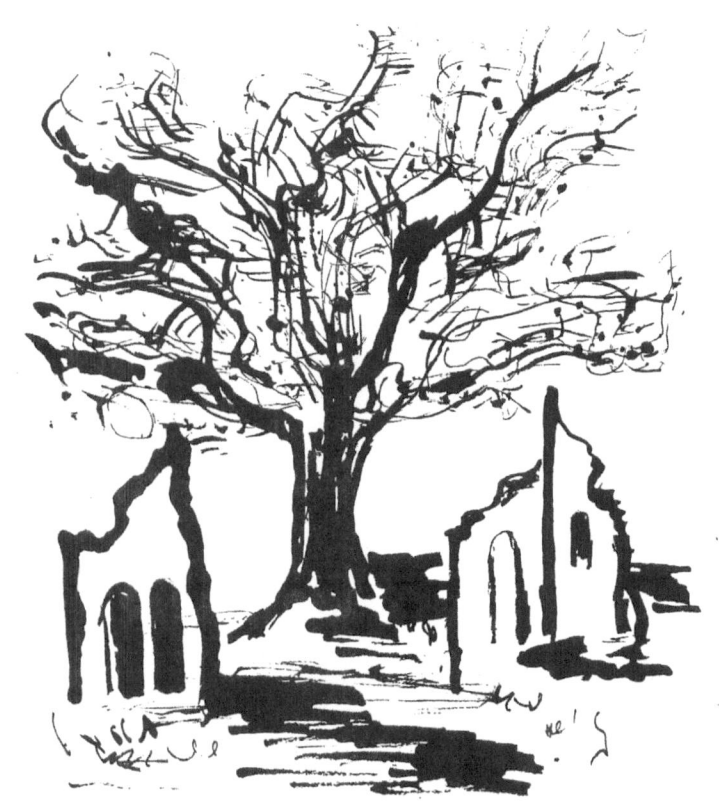

Out of the ruins,
out of mid-winter;
flowering!

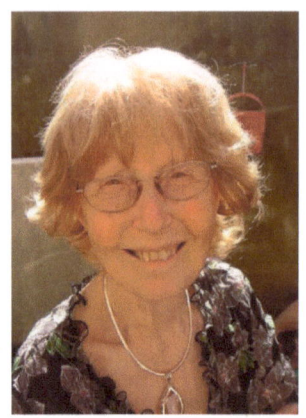

ABOUT THE AUTHOR

Tessa Lorant Warburg was born in Germany but moved to England with her family at an early age. She still lives in England - with her elder son, his Thai wife and their three lively children.

Tessa obtained a University of London BA in Mathematics, then moved to the United States for her first job. She worked as a computer programmer in New York City, then left to teach Pure Mathematics at the University of Wisconsin while working for her AM degree there. She married Jeremy Warburg, then she and her husband returned to England where their three children were born.

The young family moved to the Somerset Levels in the nineteen sixties. Tessa, entranced by the landscape around her, spent several years painting as well as growing all the family's fruit and vegetables. Then, encouraged by her husband, she began her literary career by writing on knitting.

Tessa has always had a keen interest in knitting, initiated by her University tutor, a geometer, who pointed out the connection between knitting and topology.

Her first manuscript was immediately taken up by Batsford, another by Van Nostrand Reinhold. She then began work on *The Heritage of Knitting* titles, published by The Thorn Press. All these titles sold particularly well. Tessa is written up in Richard Rutt's seminal *A History of Hand Knitting*.

Tessa began to broaden her writing. At her late husband's request she wrote *A Voice at Twilight* (Peter Owen, 1988), a book about her husband's last year as a cancer patient. It won the OddFellows Social Concern Award for 1988.

Several novels followed: three chillers published by Headline and co-written with her daughter Madeleine under the name Emma Lorant.

Bearing in mind the success of the *Heritage of Knitting* books, Tessa decided to revive The Thorn Press, the independent imprint founded by her late husband. She started by publishing *The Dohlen Inheritance*, a trilogy based on her mother's family which hailed from North Germany.

Since then Tessa has published three more novels: *Spellbinder, Thou Shalt Not Kill* and *The Girl from the Land of Smiles*, all available as paperbacks and e-books. She has also published books by local authors.

Tessa continues to run The Thorn Press, publishing a select number of books. She also continues to write both fiction and nonfiction.

Tessa writes under several names to distinguish the writing genres. She uses the name Tessa Lorant Warburg for her mainstream writing, Tessa Lorant for her craft books and co-authored books, Emma Lorant for her scifi fiction written with her daughter Madeleine Warburg, and 'teil' for her paintings and books about her paintings.

OTHER BOOKS BY THE SAME AUTHOR

FICTION

CLONER, formerly CRADLE OF SECRETS
LULLABY OF FEAR
BABY ROULETTE

THE DOHLEN INHERITANCE trilogy:
THE DOHLEN INHERITANCE
HOBGOBLIN GOLD
LADYBIRD FLY

SPELLBINDER
THOU SHALT NOT KILL
THE GIRL FROM THE LAND OF SMILES

NONFICTION

A VOICE AT TWILIGHT (Diary of a Dying Man), Winner of the ODD FELLOWS Social Concern
Book Award 1989.
THE GROCKLES' GUIDE (with Jeremy Warburg)
SNACK YOURSELF SLIM (with Richard J Warburg)

KNITTING BOOKS

THE BATSFORD BOOK OF HAND AND MACHINE KNITTING
THE BATSFORD BOOK OF HAND AND MACHINE KNITTED LACES
YARNS FOR TEXTILE CRAFTS

EARNING AND SAVING WITH A KNITTING MACHINE
CHOOSING AND BUYING A KNITTING MACHINE
YARNS FOR THE KNITTER
THE GOOD YARN GUIDE

THE HERITAGE OF KNITTING SERIES

TESSA LORANT'S COLLECTION OF KNITTED LACE EDGINGS
KNITTED QUILTS AND FLOUNCES, REPUBLISHED IN 2012
KNITTED LACE COLLARS
KNITTED SHAWLS AND WRAPS
THE SECRETS OF SUCCESSFUL IRISH CROCHET LACE
KNITTED LACE DOILIES

ALL BOOKS ARE AVAILABLE FROM Amazon worldwide
enquiries@thethornpress.com

THE THORN PRESS

BOOKS IN PRINT

The Dohlen Inheritance trilogy - Tessa Lorant Warburg
The Dohlen Inheritance
Paperback: ISBN 978-0-906374-06-1
Hardback: ISBN 978-0-906374-03-0
Hobgoblin Gold
Paperback: ISBN 978-0-906374-08-4
Ladybird Fly
Paperback: ISBN 978-0-906374-09-2

A Woman's World, 138-9 Chri Plus, Hilary Jerome
Paperback: ISBN 978-0-906374-00-9
e-book, ISBN 978-0-906374-27-6

Snack Yourself Slim, Richard Warburg & Tessa Lorant
Paperback: ISBN 978-0-906374-05-4
e-book, ISBN 978-0-906374-38-2

Inktastic, Andrew P Jones
Paperback: ISBN 978-0-906374-04-7

The Master's Tale, A Titanic Ghost Story, Ann Victoria Roberts
Paperback: ISBN 978-0-906374-21-4
e-book, ISBN 978-0-906374-39-9

Wordfall, The 2010 Anthology from Southampton Writing Buddies
Editor Penny Legg
Paperback: ISBN 978-0-906374-26-9

Knitted Quilts & Flounces, Tessa Lorant
Paperback: ISBN 978-0-906374-29-0

Spellbinder, Tessa Lorant Warburg
Paperback: ISBN 978-0-906374-31-3
e-book, ISBN 978-0-906374-35-1

Thou Shalt Not Kill, Tessa Lorant Warburg
Paperback: ISBN 978-0-906374-28-3
e-book, ISBN 978-0-906374-34-4

The Girl From The Land of Smiles, Tessa Lorant Warburg
Proverbs translated by Praphaphorn Phonbuakai
Paperback: ISBN 978-0-906374-30-6
e-book, ISBN 978-0-906374-41-2

Brushstrokes to Sponges, Richard Warburg
Hardback: ISBN 978-0-906374-43-6
Paperback: ISBN 978-0-906374-40-5
e-book: ISBN 978-0-906374-42-9

All books are available from Amazon worldwide, and from good book shops
www.thethornpress.com

www.ingramcontent.com/pod-product-compliance
Lightning Source LLC
Chambersburg PA
CBHW050818180526
45159CB00004B/1712